Quotations
from the Wayside

Edited by
Brenda Wong

Skinner House Books
Boston

Copyright © 1999 by the Unitarian Universalist Association,
25 Beacon Street, Boston, MA 02108-2800. All rights reserved.

Printed in the USA.
ISBN 1-55896-373-1

Cover design by Sue Charles.
Text design by Suzanne Morgan.

10 9 8 7 6 5 4 3 2 1
02 01 00 99

CONTENTS

INTRODUCTION

More than forty years ago, a despondent Korean War veteran stood on the Brooklyn Bridge ready to jump. His suicidal mood was brought up short when he remembered a message he had seen posted outside his neighborhood church. It read: "When you come to the end of your rope—tie a knot in it and hang on."

The man decided to hang on to life because of hope offered by a bulletin board. Roadside messages like the one he remembered once dotted church grounds in 500 cities on four continents. How this tradition began can be traced to two differing tales, one starting in Massachusetts and the other in England.

The roadside bulletin board was first introduced to North American churches in 1919 by Henry Hallam Saunderson, minister of the First Parish Church (Unitarian) of Brighton, Massachusetts, and secretary of the American Unitarian Association's publicity department from 1915 to 1921. Saunderson noticed that "many bulletin boards in front of churches were ineffectual because they were either kept empty or held notices which had outlived their usefulness." Inspired by the local wayside shrines he had seen in Europe, he decided to create "wayside sermons," liberal messages that would make people stop, read, and search their conscience.

Saunderson started by posting brief quotations each Sunday night on the bulletin board outside his church. When hundreds of people stopped to read the messages, he decided the idea might have a wider usefulness. After Saunderson polled various clergy in the area, one hundred ministers agreed to subscribe to his wayside sermons. Subscribers would erect bulletin boards of the same size and proportion on their church grounds and share the expense of having weekly messages printed on 32 x 44 inch sheets that would be readable from across the street. At one point, twelve different denominations subscribed to the service, including Presbyterian, Baptist, United Church of Christ, and Episcopal churches.

These message boards became known as the Wayside Community Pulpit, reaching as many as three million readers, according to a 1924 poll. During the subscription's early conception, Saunderson composed each weekly message. When the American Unitarian Association picked up on Saunderson's idea, it culled quotations from the world's literature, and, in 1956, expanded their scope to include contributions from ministers and laypeople.

The wayside message was first introduced to British churches by the Reverend H. Harrold Johnson. Called in 1919 to bring new life into the declining Cross Street Chapel in Manchester, Johnson created the Wayside Pulpit "Thought for the Week," pithy messages that would appeal to the person in the street, rather than the person in the pew. These messages were hand painted on 40 x 30 inch posters and were changed each week. The first Wayside Pulpit was posted on December 26, 1920, for all of Manchester to see. From that day on, a new poster appeared every Sunday morning for the next fifty years. Even when England was blitzed during World War II and the Chapel stood roofless, a weekly message appeared. The legacy of Wayside Pulpits in England is carried on by the General Assembly of Unitarian and Free Christian Churches.

In North America, the Wayside tradition continued under the Unitarian Universalist Association, which was created in 1961 when the American Unitarian Association and the Universalist Church of America merged. Between 1963 and 1977, the Wayside Community Pulpit struggled to survive against changing sentiments and rising manufacturing costs. The number of Wayside subscribers had dwindled to 220 in 1968. More people viewed the Wayside Community Pulpit as an identification of a Unitarian Universalist church, rather than as a good message to be widely used. Many non-Unitarian Universalist churches agreed with the idea of the service, but didn't always agree with the liberal content of the quotations.

By 1982, the frequency of the publication decreased from one quotation per week to one quotation every ten days. In 1986, it shrank to twenty-six quotations once a year. By 1989, the service was reduced to a set of quotations every two years. That is how it exists today.

This collection contains quotations from the Wayside tradition started in North America. Research into historical Wayside correspondence reveals that there had long been demand for a print collection of the quotations. One attempt was made in 1976, but the result was only a small pamphlet of fifty or so quotes from the last quarter century.

Like the 1976 pamphlet, this collection isn't necessarily the best of the Wayside Pulpit, but, as Wayside editor Meredith Webb wrote in 1975, "I hope it will not be considered the worst of Wayside." *Quotations from the Wayside* differs from traditional quotation books because its contents were honed from years of liberal religion. This liberal message is reflected in many of the quotations and in the categories chosen here. Included are the few Saunderson quotes that survived in the Unitarian Universalist Association archives, and much material compiled by past Wayside Pulpit editors.

When Henry Hallam Saunderson created the first Wayside Community Pulpit in North America in 1919, he thought to spread a little liberal thinking by publishing thought-provoking messages that reflect universal truths. These messages are the essence of Saunderson's legacy, a hope to find the divine in ourselves. May we be so inspired.

WORKING AROUND SEXIST LANGUAGE

The quotations in this collection are reprinted as they originally appeared in the Wayside Community Pulpit and may contain language considered sexist or archaic by today's standards. To preserve history as it was written, I have left them as they are. But I offer the following tips developed by Rosalie Maggio, compiler of *The Beacon Book of Quotations*, to make the quotes more inclusive for your use.

- Use quotation marks for part of the quotation that does not contain sexist or archaic language, and rewrite the rest.
- Use brackets or ellipses to omit sexist or archaic material.
- Use "[sic]" to indicate the material was sexist in the original and draw your reader's attention to the inaccuracy.
- When a quotation is tightly woven with sexist words, credit the writer for the idea, omitting the quotation marks and rephrasing the words.

Every effort has been made to properly credit the quotations in this book. Errors made in the past, however, are sometimes carried into the future. If you have corrections, please write to Skinner House Books, 25 Beacon Street, Boston, Massachusetts 02108-2800.

ACTION/ACTIVISM

So do your work in the world that others may do their work better.

FELIX ADLER

Let yourself and not your words preach for you.

HENRI FREDERIC AMIEL

Stand and silently watch the world go by—and it will.

ANONYMOUS

Everyone is taking a stand these days and so there is a lot of standing around.

JAMES BEVEL

To think of God all the time is to preclude doing the will of God.

E. S. BRIGHTMAN

All service ranks the same with God—there is no last or first.

ROBERT BROWNING

All that is necessary for the triumph of evil is that good men do nothing.

EDMUND BURKE

The best way to keep good acts in memory is to refresh them with new.

CATO

May your life preach more loudly than your lips.

WILLIAM ELLERY CHANNING

God heeds not what we say, but what we are and what we do.

WILLIAM ELLERY CHANNING

It is better to light a candle than to curse the darkness.

CHINESE PROVERB

If I cannot do great things, I can do small things in a great way.

JAMES FREEMAN CLARKE

Trouble neglected becomes still more troublesome.

CONFUCIUS

A good example is like a bell that calls many to church.

DANISH PROVERB

The immediate reward of noble action is that it lifts a man above himself.

ERNEST DIMNET

Where there is so much to be done . . . there must be something for me to do.

If there is no struggle, there is no progress.

The destiny of mankind hangs in the balance of what we say and what we accomplish.

There is no limit to what can be accomplished if it doesn't matter who gets the credit.

The brothers should preach by their works.

Plough deep while sluggards sleep.

Every word is vain that is not completed by deed.

Ability is useless unless it is used.

In our era the road to holiness necessarily passes through the world of action.

Religious ends are in need of our deeds.

ABRAHAM HESCHEL

To remain aloof is to die before one begins to live.

WILLIAM E. HOCKING

An idea is a curious thing. It will not work unless you do.

JAEGER'S FACTS

I will show thee my faith by my works.

JAMES 2:18

The service of the highest is a cosmic patriotism which calls for volunteers.

WILLIAM JONES

Now is the time come; let it not pass unused.

JAVANESE INSCRIPTION

Let us not love in word or speech, but in deed and in truth.

I JOHN 3:18

Genius begins great works; labor alone finishes them.

JOSEPH JOUBERT

You are what you do, not what you say you'll do.

CARL JUNG

When your work speaks for itself, don't interrupt.

HENRY J. KAISER

It is not what happens to me that makes me great, but what I do.

KIERKEGAARD

Men are brothers in good deeds regardless of their different creeds.

PHILIP M. LARSON

You become what you do, not what you think.

EDUARD LINDEMAN

It is labor that puts the difference of value on everything.

JOHN LOCKE

Live and let live is not enough; live and help live is not too much.

ORIN E. MADISON

Small deeds done are better than great deeds planned.

PETER MARSHALL

People who look too long upon evil without opposing it go dead inside.

AGNES E. MEYER

To forbear doing is often as noble as to do.

MICHEL DE MONTAIGNE

Pray for the dead and fight like hell for the living.

MOTHER JONES

It is not how much we do, but how much love we put in the doing.

MOTHER TERESA

Do good with what thou hast, or it will do thee no good.

WILLIAM PENN

Liberty is not permission to withdraw from the world's battles.

H. L. SHORT

Words are so easy; action is so difficult.

ADLAI E. STEVENSON

Wishing and hoping avail little. Only action pays.

L. C. STECKLE

Our failure to choose may become the choice we have to live with.

ROBERT STEIN

We do not have to wait until we are excellent before we can do excellent things.

PIERRE TEILHARD DE CHARDIN

Be not simply good; be good for something.

HENRY DAVID THOREAU

The dictionary is the only place where success comes before work.

ABIGAIL VAN BUREN

There are two ways of spreading light: to be the candle or the mirror that reflects it.

EDITH WHARTON

ADVENTURE

Go out on a limb. That's where the fruit is.

ANONYMOUS

Adventure is not outside a man; it is within.

DAVID GRAYSON

A ship is safe in a harbor, but that is not what a ship is for.

RALPH HELVERSON

Without adventure, civilization is in full decay.

ALFRED NORTH WHITEHEAD

AGING

Everyone is too old for something, but no one is too old for everything.

ANONYMOUS

We grow neither better nor worse as we get old, but more like ourselves.

MAY LEMBERTON BECKER

To be old is a glorious thing when one has not un-learned what it means to begin.

MARTIN BUBER

The years teach much which the days never know.

RALPH WALDO EMERSON

Youth and age touch only the surface of our lives.

C. S. LEWIS

As life grows briefer, I must make it grow deeper.

MICHEL DE MONTAIGNE

The quickest way to become an old dog is to stop learning new tricks.

CY N. PEASE

CHANGE

For a thought to change the world, it must first change the life of the person who carries it.

ALBERT CAMUS

Cleanse out the old leaven that you may be fresh dough.

I CORINTHIANS 5:7

Every reform was once a private opinion.

RALPH WALDO EMERSON

You have to live by shedding.

ROBERT FROST

Only that which changes remains true.

CARL JUNG

A stream stays alive by moving.

PHILIP M. LARSON, JR.

Perhaps we never appreciate the here and now until it is challenged.

ANNE MORROW LINDBERGH

To live is to change, and to be perfect is to have changed often.

CARDINAL NEWMAN

When things are breaking up, something great is breaking through.

VIVIAN T. POMEROY

To understand is to change, and to go beyond oneself.

JEAN-PAUL SARTRE

The world's best reformers are those who begin on themselves.

GEORGE BERNARD SHAW

Habits are at first cobwebs then cables.

SPANISH PROVERB

Let the great world spin for ever down the ringing grooves of change.

TENNYSON

Loyalty to petrified opinions never yet broke a chain.

MARK TWAIN

All orthodoxies began by being heresies.

UNAMUNO Y JUGO

CHARACTER

It is not in the still calm of life that great characters are formed.

ABIGAIL ADAMS

The workshop of character is everyday life.

ANONYMOUS

Good character is not formed at the New Year.

MALTBIE D. BABCOCK

You grow up the day you have your first real laugh at yourself.

ETHEL BARRYMORE

Temperament we are born with; character we have to make.

J. BALDWIN BROWN

The perfection of virtue comes of struggle.

MEISTER ECKHART

It is very hard to be simple enough to be good.

RALPH WALDO EMERSON

Man's character is his fate.

HERACLITUS

The noblest worship is to make yourself as good and as just as you can.

ISOCRATES

Character is what you are in the dark.

DWIGHT L. MOODY

Contemporary reputations make fragile future pedestals.

CHARLES NORMAN

Swallow your pride occasionally. It is non-fattening.

RAPID SERVICE 66

At the end, one has the face that one earned.

MAX RODEN

Most people have to talk so they won't hear.

MAY SARTON

Character is a priceless fabric which the unseen fingers of the soul are ever weaving.

HENRY H. SAUNDERSON

Character is what you are; reputation, what people think you are.

HENRY H. SAUNDERSON

It is listening, not silence, that shows respect.

J. FRANK SCHULMAN

Shallow brooks murmur most.

SIR PHILIP SIDNEY

Only humility can never be humiliated.

HOWARD THURMAN

Everybody thinks of changing humanity and nobody thinks of changing themselves.

LEO TOLSTOY

CHILDREN

Give us a child's faith, that we may be cured of our cynicism.

SARA MOORES CAMPBELL

The child is the best symbol of the creative fire in man.

SUSANNAH COOLIDGE

Each night a child is born is a holy night.

SOPHIA LYON FAHS

Children have more need of models than of critics.

JOSEPH JOUBERT

If help and salvation are to come, they can only come from the children.

MARIE MONTESSORI

It often happens that the saints are wrong and the children of the world are right.

GILBERT MURRAY

A baby is God's opinion that the world should go on.

CARL SANDBURG

Every child comes with the message that God is not yet discouraged of man.

RABINDRANATH TAGORE

CONSCIENCE

Reason, Conscience—by which we discover the true and the right are immortal as their author.

WILLIAM ELLERY CHANNING

The only guide to a man is his conscience.

SIR WINSTON CHURCHILL

I have never been hurt by anything I didn't say.

CALVIN COOLIDGE

Crime and punishment grow out of one stem.

RALPH WALDO EMERSON

I'd rather take a beating from a mob than from my conscience.

JOSEPHINE GABRIELLE

Conscience is the internal testimony which we bear to ourselves.

PAUL D'HOLBACH

Courage without conscience is a wild beast.

R. G. INGERSOLL

Whatever is rightly done, however humble, is noble.

SIR HENRY ROYCE

The head does not hear anything until the heart has listened.

JAMES STEPHENS

CONVICTION AND BELIEF

The seat of ethics is in our hearts, not in our minds.

VANNEVAR BUSH

There is no mistake so great as that of being always right.

SAMUEL BUTLER

We must train not only the head, but the heart and the hand.

MADAME CHIANG KAI-SHEK

Nothing can bring you peace but the triumph of principles.

RALPH WALDO EMERSON

Some things have to be believed to be seen.

RALPH HODGSON

Every calling is great when greatly pursued.

OLIVER WENDELL HOLMES

Make your word more reliable than the oaths of others.

ISOCRATES

The vows one makes privately are more binding than any ceremony.

BEATRICE LILLIE

Convictions are more dangerous enemies of truth than lies.

FRIEDRICH NIETZSCHE

An army of principles will penetrate where an army of soldiers cannot.

THOMAS PAINE

Beliefs are really rules for action.

CHARLES SANDERS PEIRCE

Keep thy heart with diligence; from it come the issues of life.

PROVERBS 4:23

God is dead unless his people speak.

ROBERT REED

What we need is not the will to believe, but the wish to find out.

BERTRAND RUSSELL

We believe without belief, beyond belief.

WALLACE STEVENS

Who leads us is less important than what leads us.

ADLAI E. STEVENSON

Goodness is the only investment that never fails.

HENRY DAVID THOREAU

Doubts are the things that unite mankind; convictions separate them.

PETER USTINOV

It is not facts but our beliefs about facts which control our actions.

JOHN F. WHARTON

COURAGE

I'm not afraid of storms, for I'm learning how to sail my ship.

LOUISA MAY ALCOTT

The healthy, strong individual is the one who asks for help when he or she needs it.

RONA BARRETT (ADAPTED)

In the midst of winter I discovered that there was in me an invincible summer.

ALBERT CAMUS

Courage means using our utmost energies to secure worthwhile ends.

MORRIS RAPHAEL COHEN

Behold the turtle: he makes progress only when he sticks his neck out.

JAMES BRYANT CONANT

Courage is the conquest of fear, not the absence of it.

A. POWELL DAVIES

Courage is the price that Life exacts for granting peace.

AMELIA EARHART

What a new face courage puts on everything!

RALPH WALDO EMERSON

We have to stumble and fall if we are to walk.

SAMUEL H. MILLER

The pursuit of truth is a form of courage.

GEORGE SANTAYANA

DIVERSITY

God hath made of one blood all nations of men for to
dwell upon all the face of the earth.

ACTS 17:26

Where diversity is suppressed, blasphemy and distor-
tion ensue.

JAMES LUTHER ADAMS

All people smile in the same language.

ANONYMOUS

Surely there is enough space in all the world for all.

TAYLOR CALDWELL

We must judge others not by our light but by their
own.

WILLIAM ELLERY CHANNING

You need not think alike to love alike.

FRANCIS DÁVID

Tolerance is the finest flower of civilization and the last
to bloom.

MARSHALL DAWSON

Harmony exists in difference no less than in likeness.

MARGARET FULLER

A community without dissent is well on the way to becoming an ant heap.

FRED HOYLE

Diversity is the best defense of healthy societies.

GEORGE KENNAN

It is important that human beings shall be united, but not that they shall be uniform.

ASHLEY MONTAGU

Accomplishments have no color.

LEONTYNE PRICE

A clash of doctrines is not a disaster; it is an opportunity.

ALFRED NORTH WHITEHEAD

The worth of an individual is not related to the color of his or her skin.

WHITNEY MOORE YOUNG, JR.

DOGMA

The dogmas of the past are inadequate to the stormy present.

ABRAHAM LINCOLN

We live in a world so full of responsibility that dogma-tism is simply indecent.

HARRY MESERVE

The assurance of dogma, the arrogance of certainty, are enemies of wisdom.

FREDERICK RUDOLPH

DOUBT

True doubt is not unfaith, but the critical act of faith in quest of truth.

ANONYMOUS

Scepticism is the first step to philosophy.

DENIS DIDEROT

Doubt is the whetstone of understanding.

JOHN DOS PASSOS

He is without faith who is afraid of doubters.

J. DONALD JOHNSTON

Fanaticism is always a compensation for hidden doubt.

CARL JUNG

The depth of man's questioning is more important than his answers.

ANDRÉ MALRAUX

The only limit to our realization of tomorrow will be our doubts of today.

FRANKLIN D. ROOSEVELT

Modest doubt is called the beacon of the wise.

WILLIAM SHAKESPEARE

Faith and doubt, both are needed.

LILLIAN SMITH

There lives more faith in honest doubt than in half the creeds.

TENNYSON

FAITH

An unexamined faith is not worth having.

JAMES LUTHER ADAMS

The best of our knowledge is but a faith.

JAMES AGEE

To choose what is difficult all one's days as if it were easy, that is faith.

W. H. AUDEN

Faith cannot be recommended; it can only be called upon.

HENRY G. BEYBEE, JR.

The written code kills, but the Spirit gives life.
II CORINTHIANS 3:6

The faith that stands on authority is not faith.
RALPH WALDO EMERSON

Faith cannot be circumscribed by dogma.
GEOFFREY HEAD

Faith is not an abstraction but a way of living.
PALFREY PERKINS

Thy word is a lamp to my feet and a light to my path.
PSALMS 119:105

The weakest faith is that which fears to doubt.
J. FRANK SCHULMAN

Faith has nothing to fear from thinking.
ALBERT SCHWEITZER

The present chaotic stage is not caused by lack of faith, but by too much unreasoning faith.
GEORGE SIMPSON

Faith is the subtle chain which binds us to the infinite.
ELIZABETH OAKES SMITH

On your lonely path may you not walk alone.
HOWARD THURMAN

Neither by strength nor by might but by my spirit, saith the Lord.

ZECHARIAH 4:6

FORGIVENESS

Help us, O God, through others' faults to their needs.

ANONYMOUS

It is difficult indeed to forgive a man for not forgiving you.

TIMOTHY HUME BEHRENDT

To forgive is wisdom; to forget is genius.

JOYCE CARY

Love is not real until forgiveness is real.

JOHN F. HAYWARD

We forgive to the extent that we love.

LA ROCHEFOUCAULD

The man whom society will not forgive nor restore is driven into recklessness.

F. W. ROBERTSON

It is in giving that we receive, it is in pardoning that we are pardoned.

ST. FRANCIS OF ASSISI

The unforgivable sin is the refusal to pardon.

GEORGE SANTAYANA

The heart has always the pardoning power.

ANNE SWETCHINE

Love is an act of endless forgiveness.

PETER USTINOV

FREEDOM

Resistance to tyranny is obedience to God.

SUSAN B. ANTHONY

It is a strange desire to seek power and lose liberty.

FRANCIS BACON

Freedom is the fire which burns away illusion.

JAMES BALDWIN

If our brothers are oppressed, then we are oppressed.

STEPHEN VINCENT BENET

Grant us faith and understanding to cherish all those
who fight for freedom.

STEPHEN VINCENT BENET

The liberty of all is necessary for the liberty of each.

H. J. BLACKMAN

Let us hold fast to the right of private judgment.

WILLIAM ELLERY CHANNING

Freedom without consecration is only another form of slavery.

FREDERICK MAY ELIOT

A slave is someone who cannot speak their thought.

EURIPIDES

Without freedom of expression, liberty of thought is a mockery.

FELIX FRANKFURTER

Freedom is to be in possession of oneself.

HEGEL

Man's ability to surpass himself is the essence of freedom.

ABRAHAM HESCHEL

Essentially, freedom means becoming more ambiguous.

IVAN ILLICH

No man is good enough to govern another man without that other man's consent.

ABRAHAM LINCOLN

The best security for freedom in any society is to practice it.

JOSEPH R. MORRAY

When you enslave someone, you are enslaved.

LOUISE NEVELSON

They alone are truly secure who ask not to be safe, but free.

W. W. ROSE

It is madness to abolish freedom because some abuse it.

HAROLD SCOTT

Freedom of each to utter means freedom of all to learn.

WAITSTILL SHARP

Emancipation means equal status for different roles.

ARIANNA STASSINOPOULOS

The annihilation of the individual is the worst perversity of man.

W. L. SULLIVAN

What is the value of political freedom but as a means to moral freedom?

HENRY DAVID THOREAU

To be deprived of freedom is to become either a chattel or an animal.

J. E. TURNER

We don't want our chains made more bearable. We want our chains removed.

ARCHBISHOP DESMOND TUTU

The liberty you possess is the work of common dangers, sufferings, and successes.

GEORGE WASHINGTON

GIVING

Fragrance always stays in the hand that gives the rose.

HADA BEJAR

Real generosity toward the future lies in giving all to the present.

ALBERT CAMUS

One who gives quickly gives twice.

CERVANTES

We make a living by what we get, we make a life by what we give.

WINSTON CHURCHILL

And now abideth faith, hope, charity, these three; but the greatest of these is charity.

I CORINTHIANS 13:13

The only gift is a portion of thyself.

RALPH WALDO EMERSON

Once you have helped another human being, you will never again be lonely.

ROBERT HENRY HOLMES

True compassion is more than flinging coins to a beggar.

MARTIN LUTHER KING, JR.

Give what you have. To someone it may be better than you dare to think.

HENRY WADSWORTH LONGFELLOW

Unto whomsoever much is given, of him shall much be required.

LUKE 12:48

Men are judged by what is given, not what is withheld.

THEODORE PARKER

Above all things have fervent charity among yourselves: for charity covers a multitude of sins.

I PETER 4:8

Rich gifts wax poor when givers prove unkind.

WILLIAM SHAKESPEARE

To help his fellow man is man's most noble work.

SOPHOCLES

We are rich only through what we give, and poor only through what we keep.

ANNE SWETCHINE

Without the abundance of the heart nothing great can happen.

PAUL TILLICH

GOD

God is no bulwark to the arrogant who spurn the great altar of God's justice.

AESCHYLUS

We do too narrowly define the power of God, restraining it to our capacities.

ANONYMOUS

Without God we cannot; without us God will not.

ST. AUGUSTINE

If you hallow this life, you meet the living God.

MARTIN BUBER

God listens to the heart, not to words.

GASTON M. CARRIER

Do you not know that you are God's temple and that God's Spirit dwells in you?

I CORINTHIANS 3:16

Where the Spirit of the Lord is, there is freedom.

II CORINTHIANS 3:17

You can't find God before an altar if that is the only place you look for him.

A. POWELL DAVIES

This something that we call God is the indwelling idealism of humanity.

DURANT DRAKE

To seek God by rituals is to get the ritual and lose God in the process.

MEISTER ECKHART

God offers the choice between truth and repose. Take which you please—you can never have both.

RALPH WALDO EMERSON

God enters by a private door into every individual.

RALPH WALDO EMERSON

Try first thyself, and after, call in God; for to the
worker God lends aid.

EURIPIDES

Wherever souls of men have worshipped, there is God.

HERBERT D. GALLAUDET

The God who gave us life gave us liberty at the same
time.

THOMAS JEFFERSON

God enters the world in every man.

WILLIAM B. KILLAM

God is as close to us as we are to ourselves.

MARJORIE NEWLIN LEAMING

The search for God is the search for reality.

SIDNEY E. MEAD

All things proceed from God; all things end in God.

GEORGE MOORE

You love God best when you love men most.

THEODORE PARKER

The Lord is my strength and my song, and is become
my salvation.

PSALM 118:14

Every picture of God is a self-portrait.

J. FRANK SCHULMAN

God is not against us for our sins. God is for us against our sins.

DAVID A. SEAMANDS

HATE

There is no medicine for hate.

AFRICAN PROVERB

A man's venom poisons himself more than his victims.

CHARLES BUXTON

Leave hate to those who are too weak to love.

MICHEL DEL CASTILLO

Never does hatred cease by hating in return.

DHAMMAPADA

Let not the sun go down upon your wrath.

EPHESIANS 4:26

An eye for an eye only ends in making the whole world blind.

MOHANDAS K. GANDHI

When one is hating, he cannot be loving.

CHARLES G. GOMILLION

Whosoever hateth his brother is a murderer.

I JOHN 3:15

Better is a dinner of herbs where love is, than a stalled ox and hatred therewith.

PROVERBS 15:17

In hatred as in love, we grow like the thing we brood upon.

MARY RENAULT

Hate is a prolonged form of suicide.

HEINRICH SCHILLER

I am determined that no man shall drag me down by making me hate him.

BOOKER T. WASHINGTON

Hate and mistrust are the children of blindness.

WILLIAM WATSON

HOPE

In each beginning an end is seen. In each end a beginning gleams.

JESSE ROY DOM

Sunset is the promise of dawn.

HAVELOCK ELLIS

One cannot cure if one knows only disease.

ERIK H. ERIKSON

Beginnings are opportunities for making endings better.

L. ANNIE FOERSTER

We are all prisoners but some of us are in cells with windows and some without.

KAHLIL GIBRAN

A possibility is a hint from God.

KIERKEGAARD

Hope that endures becomes a hope fulfilled.

JOHN MASEFIELD

Blessed are those who dream, for some of their dreams will come true.

HARRY MESERVE

There are so many dawns that have not yet spread their glow.

RIG VEDA

In a dark time, the eye begins to see.

THEODORE ROETHKE

Somewhere something incredible is waiting to happen.

CARL SAGAN

Each day comes bearing gifts. Untie the ribbons.

ANN RUTH SCHNABAKER

Hope is giving eyes to sorrow.

HARRY B. SCHOLEFIELD

At times our own light goes out and is rekindled by a spark from another.

ALBERT SCHWEITZER

To travel hopefully is a better thing than to arrive.

NEVIL SHUTE

People are best united not by mutual fear, but by mutual hope.

ADLAI E. STEVENSON

I believe in the sun even when it is not shining.

WARSAW GHETTO VICTIM

HUMANITY

I am a human being. Do not fold, spindle, or mutilate.

ANONYMOUS

Our humanity were a poor thing but for the divinity
that stirs in us.

FRANCIS BACON

Love is the weaver; the threads are living folk.

RAYMOND BAUGHAN

We may not know what God is, but we can know what it
means to be human.

PAUL CARNES

This country is entrusted by God with a mission for
humanity.

WILLIAM ELLERY CHANNING

Please don't criticize me for being human. It's my most
redeeming feature.

CYNTHIA J. GOULD

To be human is not a fact, but a task.

FREDERICK H. HEINEMANN

With malice toward none; with charity for all; let us
strive on to finish the work we are in.

ABRAHAM LINCOLN

We never move toward the divine by ignoring the
human.

WILLIAM LYNCH

It's great to be great, but greater to be human.

WILL ROGERS

Search and see if there is not some place where you may invest your humanity.

ALBERT SCHWEITZER

Humanitarianism consists in never sacrificing a human being to a purpose.

ALBERT SCHWEITZER

There is a common humanity that transcends all differences in dogma.

GEORGE STODDARD

There is nothing so threatening to humanity as humanity itself.

LEWIS THOMAS

IN MEMORIAM

At the going down of the sun and in the morning we will remember them.

LAWRENCE BINYON

Their bodies are buried in peace, but their name liveth forevermore.

ECCLESIASTICUS 44:14

In the remembrance of a glorious past, individuals and nations find their noblest inspiration.

SIR WILLIAM OSLER

Death is only a horizon; and a horizon is nothing save the limit of our sight.

ROSSITER W. RAYMOND

INTERDEPENDENCE

Each man is as much an inhabitant of the earth as he is of his country.

HANNAH ARENDT

The blossoms of today draw strength from the roots of a thousand years ago.

JAPANESE POEM

I can never be what I ought to be until you are what you ought to be.

MARTIN LUTHER KING, JR.

Whether we wish it or not, we are involved in the world's problems.

WALTER LIPPMAN

Man was not created to preside over all other creatures, but to live in harmony with them.

ASHLEY MONTAGU

I feel we are all islands—in a common sea.

ANNE MORROW LINDBERGH

As God dwells in all creatures, none is to be despised.

RAMANANDA

Live together, talk together, walk together. We are all One.

SWAMI SATYANANDA

We did not weave the web of life: We are merely a strand in it.

CHIEF SEATTLE

Those who are most vigorous in rejecting the past are also most careless of the future.

MARY MCDERMOTT SHIDELER

With all beings and all things we shall be as relatives.

SIOUX INDIAN

Though leaves are many, the root is one.

WILLIAM BUTLER YEATS

INTOLERANCE

Prejudice delivers instant opinions without bothering with all those facts.

ANONYMOUS

He who never changes his mind never corrects his errors.

ANONYMOUS

Prejudice is being down on what you are not up on.

MARGARET T. APPLEGARTH

If you could make all men think alike, it would be very much as if no man thought at all.

PHILLIP BROOKS

Nothing is more dangerous than an idea, when you have only one idea.

ÉMILE-AUGUSTE CHARTIER

A closed mind is like a closed book, just a block of wood.

CHINESE PROVERB

Intolerance betrays want of faith in one's cause.

MOHANDAS K. GANDHI

Prejudice is the child of ignorance.

WILLIAM HAZLITT

Drawing boundaries is the preoccupation of minds incapable of building bridges.

BRIAN HOCKING

They must first judge themselves that presume to censure others.

WILLIAM PENN

Zeal is very blind when it encroaches upon the rights of others.

P. QUESNEL

Fear is at the bottom of all intolerance.

HENDRIK WILLEM VAN LOON

JUSTICE

Let justice roll down as waters, and righteousness an overflowing stream.

AMOS 5:24

The best way of avenging thyself is not to become like the wrongdoer.

MARCUS AURELIUS

The inequalities suffered by the many are in no way justified by the rise of a few.

JAMES BALDWIN

Without justice, peace is nothing but a nice-sounding word.

DOM HELDER CAMARA

Kindness without justice is of little moral worth.

WILLIAM ELLERY CHANNING

While there's a soul in prison I am not free.

EUGENE V. DEBS

We cannot do evil to others without doing it to ourselves.

DESMAHIS

One hour of justice is worth three thousand hours of prayer.

KEMAL DJUMBLATT, LEBANESE REVOLUTIONARY LEADER

Riches that leave another poor I do not want.

ANDRÉ GIDE

Tolerance is a virtue, but indifference is a vice.

DANA MCLEAN GREELEY

We are not punished for our sins but by them.

ELBERT HUBBARD

There is nothing more tragic in all this world than to know right and not do it.

MARTIN LUTHER KING, JR.

Injustice anywhere is a threat to justice everywhere.

MARTIN LUTHER KING, JR.

No lie can live forever.

MARTIN LUTHER KING, JR.

Justice is nothing else than love felt by the wise.

LIEBNIZ

Why should there not be a patient confidence in the ultimate justice of the people?

ABRAHAM LINCOLN

To sin by silence when they should protest makes cowards out of people.

ABRAHAM LINCOLN

With what measure ye mete, it shall be measured to you again.

MATTHEW 7:12

If you want peace, work for justice.

POPE PAUL VI

Among citizens there should be no forgotten people and no forgotten races.

FRANKLIN D. ROOSEVELT

We should all take our share of the burden of pain which lies upon the world.

ALBERT SCHWEITZER

The worst sin toward our fellow creatures is not to hate them but to be indifferent to them.

GEORGE BERNARD SHAW

Justice is love operating at a distance.

JOSEPH SITTLER

The strictest justice is sometimes the greatest injustice.

TERENCE

Injustice in the end produces independence.

VOLTAIRE

Who degrades another degrades me.

WALT WHITMAN

KNOWLEDGE

All experience is an arch to build upon.

HENRY BROOKS ADAMS

The fate of empires depends on the education of youth.

ARISTOTLE

There is no money lost that is used in educating the people.

OLYMPIA BROWN

One great thought breathed into a man may regenerate him.

WILLIAM ELLERY CHANNING

Let's not think so much we forget to feel.

ROGER COWAN

Minds are like parachutes—they only function when open.

THOMAS DEWAR

Education is not preparation for life; education is life itself.

JOHN DEWEY

In much wisdom is much grief:
and he that increaseth
Knowledge increaseth sorrow.

ECCLESIASTES 12:12

The only rational way of educating is to be an example.

ALBERT EINSTEIN

Knowledge is the antidote to fear.

RALPH WALDO EMERSON

Nations die by suicide. The sign of it is the decay of thought.

RALPH WALDO EMERSON

Zeal without knowledge is fire without light.

ENGLISH PROVERB

If you have knowledge, let others light their candle at it.

MARGARET FULLER

If you do not think about the future, you cannot have one.

JOHN GALSWORTHY

There is no sight more fearful than ignorance in action.

GOETHE

Education which does not produce a free mind is not education.

JOHN GUNTHER

There is no darkness but ignorance: let us flood the world with light.

ROBERT INGERSOLL

Take from the altars of the past the fire, not the ashes.

JEAN JAUVES

There is no better ruler than wisdom—no safer guardian than justice.

THE KORAN

A free people must be a thinking people.

EVERETT DEAN MARTIN

The mind is not sex-typed.

MARGARET MEAD

It is not so important to know everything as to appreciate what we learn.

HANNAH MORE

Nothing ages people like not thinking.

CHRISTOPHER MORLEY

The mind is not a vessel to be filled, but a fire to be kindled.

PLUTARCH

Apply thy heart unto instruction, and thine ears to the words of knowledge.

PROVERBS 23:12

The true teachers are those who help us think for ourselves.

SARVEPALLI RADHAKRISHNAN

Knowledge is an island surrounded by a sea of mystery.

CHET RAYMO

Knowledge is good even if what is known is painful.

BERTRAND RUSSELL

Those who cannot remember the past are condemned to repeat it.

GEORGE SANTAYANA

Renunciation of thinking is a declaration of spiritual bankruptcy.

ALBERT SCHWEITZER

Learning and liberty march hand in hand or they do not march at all.

SIR HARTLEY SHAWCROSS

Howling is not a substitute for thinking.

ADLAI E. STEVENSON

None is poor but the person who lacks knowledge.

ABAYE TALMUD

Knowledge can be power and salvation if we have the power to use it.

ARNOLD J. TOYNBEE

Every thought is like a bell with many echoes.

WILLIAM BUTLER YEATS

LIFE

Who knows if life is a destination? Life is a journey.

ANONYMOUS

Some people say life is hard. Compared to what?

ANONYMOUS

The business of living is inspired by an effort to see things whole and steadily.

CHARLES A. BEARD

Life is so great a mystery that we need not invent others.

JOHN BURROUGHS

Be careful how you live your life for it is the only Gospel others will read.

HELDER CAMARA

Life is one long quarrel with God. But we can make up at the end.

THOMAS CARLISLE

Sometimes the thing our life misses helps more than the thing which it gets.

ALICE CARY

Life is not a vessel to be drained, but a cup to be filled.

CHINESE PROVERB

The law of life is development, not destruction.

JAMES FREEMAN CLARKE

The tragedy of life is not death, but what dies inside us
while we live.

NORMAN COUSINS

Nothing in life is to be feared—it is only to be
understood.

MARIE CURIE

The art of living lies in a fine mingling of letting go
and holding on.

HAVELOCK ELLIS

A ship ought not to be held by one anchor, nor life by
a single hope.

EPICTETUS

There is more to life than increasing its speed.

MOHANDAS K. GANDHI

Your daily life is your temple and your religion.

KAHLIL GIBRAN

To live is to adapt.

GOETHE

Our responsibility is not for life but for living.

ELIZABETH GOUDGE

Life is a school, not a bargain counter.

GRENFELL

Living is what man does with God's time.

ABRAHAM HESCHEL

The great use of life is to spend it for something that outlasts it.

WILLIAM JAMES

The test of a man's worth is not his theology but his life.

MORRIS JOSEPH

Life is what happens to us while we are making other plans.

THOMAS LAMANCE

We live, not as we wish to, but as we can.

MENANDER

What matters is not when we die but how we live.

MICHEL DE MONTAIGNE

Nothing in life has value except to do right and to fear not.

GILBERT MURRAY

Although life is all too short it can be ever so wide.

DAVID NARDI

Life is creation continuing.

NANCY NEWHALL

Clever people master life; the wise illuminate it and create fresh difficulties.

EMIL NOLDE

Man is born to live, not to prepare for life.

BORIS PASTERNAK

Live simply that others may simply live.

QUAKER PRECEPT

Life is not a dogma to be defended but a reality to be explored.

FLOYD ROSS

There is no wealth but life itself.

JOHN RUSKIN

May you live all the days of your life.

JONATHAN SWIFT

Give back life for life.

HENRY DAVID THOREAU

Our life is frittered away by detail . . . Simplify!

HENRY DAVID THOREAU

When it's time to die, let us not discover that we have never lived.

HENRY DAVID THOREAU

Trouble is the necessary salt of life without which life loses its savor.

ARNOLD J. TOYNBEE

The best way to know life is to love many things.

VINCENT VAN GOGH

Living, like studying, needs a little practice.

OCTAVIA WALDO

A rose to the living is more than sumptuous wreaths to the dead.

NIXON WATERMAN

LOVE

One may give without loving, but none can love without giving.

ANONYMOUS

Love is, above all, the gift of oneself.

JEAN ANOUILH

The love that is kindled at home expands itself over the race of man.

ASOKA

Love is stronger than hate, and life is stronger than death.

PEARL S. BUCK

I think true love is never blind but rather brings an added light.

PHOEBE CARY

Where there is great love there are always miracles.

WILLA CATHER

Love is patient and kind; love is not jealous or boastful.

I CORINTHIANS 13:4

The experience of love is the recollection of heaven.

ERWIN EDMAN

All work is empty save where there is love.

KAHLIL GIBRAN

All deep knowledge of persons can only be secured by love.

E. H. HUGHES

We have to choose between the love of power and the power of love.

A. GRAHAM IKIN

If we love one another God dwelleth in us.

I JOHN 4:12

There is no fear in love; perfect love casteth out fear.

I JOHN 4:18

Love oftimes knows no measure, but is fervent above all measure.

THOMAS A KEMPIS

Unarmed love is the most powerful force in the world.

MARTIN LUTHER KING, JR.

Love is so short, forgetting is so long.

PABLO NERUDA

Hate stirs up strife, but love covers all offenses.

PROVERBS 10:12

No heart which shuts out truth and love can be the abode of God.

SARVEPALLI RADHAKRISHNAN

Leave no claim outstanding against you except that of mutual love.

ROMANS 13:8

Love does not consist in gazing at each other, but in looking together in the same direction.

ANTOINE DE SAINT-EXUPÉRY

One can do much with hate, but even more with love.

WILLIAM SHAKESPEARE

Love is not love which alters when it alteration finds.

WILLIAM SHAKESPEARE

Love is strong as Death.

SONG OF SOLOMON 8:6

There are no words for love, only moments.

SHIFRA STEIN

God hath not given us the spirit of fear, but of power and of love.

II TIMOTHY 1:7

Where love is, there is God.

LEO TOLSTOY

Love lights more fires than hate extinguishes.

ELLA WHEELER WILCOX

MINDFULNESS

No one tests the depth of a river with both feet.

AFRICAN PROVERB

One can only forget time by making use of it.

CHARLES-PIERRE BAUDELAIRE

When those who fish can't go to sea, they mend nets.

THE BOOK OF RUNES (ADAPTED)

Nothing is ever said until someone listens.

PAUL CARNES

Nothing in all creation is so like God as stillness.

MEISTER ECKHART

He who stumbles but does not halt is hastened on his way.

GEORGE HERBERT

Today well lived makes every tomorrow a sacrament of joy.

ROBERT HENRY HOLMES

Be swift to hear, slow to speak.

JAMES 1:19

Listening silence shows more care than any rush of words.

J. DONALD JOHNSTON

To be blind is bad, but worse to have eyes and not to see.

HELEN KELLER

The great events are not our noisiest but our stillest hours.

FRIEDRICH NIETZSCHE

Let us not look back in anger, nor forward in fear, but around in awareness.

JAMES THURBER

Waiting is a window opening on many landscapes.

HOWARD THURMAN

The future is made of the same stuff as the present.

SIMONE WEIL

NATURE

If a bird sings among your branches, be not too ready to tame it.

HENRI FREDERIC AMIEL

It is only when we are aware of the earth as poetry that we truly live.

HENRY BESTON

Do no dishonor to the earth lest you dishonor the spirit of humanity.

HENRY BESTON

Earth's crammed with heaven, and every common bush afire with God.

ELIZABETH BARRETT BROWNING

The place whereon thou standest is holy ground.

EXODUS 3:5

Nature travaileth most painfully with her noblest products.

MARGARET FULLER

Grass is the forgiveness of nature—her constant benediction.

JOHN INGALLS

Nature's silence is its one remark.

ANNIE DILLARD

Spring has returned. The earth is like a child that knows poems.

RAINER MARIA RILKE

What is the use of a house if you haven't got a tolerable planet to put it on?

HENRY DAVID THOREAU

I think of man in nature as the divinest and most startling of facts.

HENRY DAVID THOREAU

Where the earth is, we are.

WALT WHITMAN

The earth remains jagged and broken only to him or her who remains jagged and broken.

WALT WHITMAN

Everything in nature is resurrection.

WILLIAM BUTLER YEATS

PARENTING

Think twice and pray three times before punishing a child.

MALTBIE D. BABCOCK

To become a father is not hard. To be a father is.

WILHELM BUSCH

You are the bows from which your children as living arrows are sent forth.

KAHLIL GIBRAN

Your children need your presence more than your presents.

JESSE JACKSON

Let parents bequeath to their children not riches but the spirit of reverence.

PLATO

PEACE

We must be at war with evil but at peace with man.

LORD ACTON

It is harder to live in peace than to die by violence.

ANONYMOUS

A space station we can build but peace on earth takes more brains.

CHARLES BALFOUR

Our hatred of war should only be excelled by our commitment to peace.

TIMOTHY HUME BEHRENDT

The war to end war will not be fought with guns.

LOWELL H. COATE

Be of one mind, live in peace; and the God of love and peace shall be with you.

II CORINTHIANS 13:11

Peace is not a foreign idea.

W. E. B. DU BOIS

Peace is a blessing, and, like most blessings, it must be earned.

DWIGHT D. EISENHOWER

May I win no victory that harms either me or my opponent.

EUSEBIUS

Our work for peace must begin within the private world of each one of us.

DAG HAMMARSKJÖLD

If we cannot agree, let us at any rate agree to differ, but let us part as friends.

MOHAMMAD ALI JINNAH

Keep thyself first in peace, and then thou wilt be able to bring others to peace.

THOMAS A KEMPIS

True peace is not merely the absence of tension; it is the presence of justice.

MARTIN LUTHER KING, JR.

If there is to be peace in the home,
There must be peace in the heart.

LAO TZU

Let us do all which may achieve a just and lasting peace among ourselves, and with all nations.

ABRAHAM LINCOLN

Blessed are the peacemakers, for they shall be called sons of God.

MATTHEW 5:9

It is an honor for a man to cease from strife.

PROVERBS 20:3

How beautiful are the dwellings of peace, where the holiness of God abideth.

ROLLO RUSSELL

Peace is the nature of God.

SWAMI SATCHIDANANDA

There is no way to peace; peace is the way.

MAURICE SCHWARTZ

Observe good faith and justice towards all nations.

GEORGE WASHINGTON

Friendship is the only cement that will ever hold the world together.

WOODROW WILSON

We should build in each heart a wall against war.

TSUTOMU YAMAGUCHI

REASON

Reason is light that God has kindled in the soul.

ARISTOTLE

Reason is the continuing adventure of the life and of the mind.

DEANE WILLIAM FERM

We can hold no faith which violates reason.

ERWIN R. GOODENOUGH

Error may be tolerated where reason is left free to combat it.

THOMAS JEFFERSON

To follow God and to obey reason are the same thing.

PLUTARCH

Reason will not triumph unless the mind is free.

ADLAI E. STEVENSON

The progress of reason is always the progress of a better understanding.

ALFRED NORTH WHITEHEAD

The function of reason is to promote the art of life.

ALFRED NORTH WHITEHEAD

RELIGION

Religion isn't worshipping what the prophets did, but doing what the prophets worshipped.

WILLIAM E. ALBERTS

Many have quarreled about religion that never practiced it.

AMERICAN PROVERB

The ideal in religion is to establish the proper balance between mind and emotion.

WALDEMAR ARGOW

The best theology would need no advocates; it would prove itself.

KARL BARTH

Man cannot approach the divine by reaching beyond the human.

MARTIN BUBER

Prayer does not change things; prayer changes people, and people change things.

LON RAY CALL

Worship is the supreme art of guiding the loyalty of the people.

STANTON COIT

In religion, as in everything else, survival is assured only by change.

HARVEY COX

Religion is indebted to the great doubters as well as to the great believers.

SAMUEL MCCHORD CROTHERS

The method of Jesus is to work from within outward.

WILLIAM WALLACE FENN

Religion is something you do, not something you wait for.

CHARLES G. FINNEY

I do not know any religion apart from human activity.

MOHANDAS K. GANDHI

Religion is a response to life, not a description of it.

LAUREL HALLMAN

It is in our lives, and not from our words, that our religion must be read.

THOMAS JEFFERSON

All great prayer is born out of intense earnestness.

RUFUS M. JONES

He who is faithful in a very little, is faithful also in much.

LUKE 16:10

Religion is a temper, not a pursuit.

HARRIET MARTINEAU

The real enemy of religion is indifference and cynicism.

TOMAS MASARYK

Prayer . . . doesn't burn up any fossil fuel, it doesn't pollute.

MARGARET MEAD

Give them, not Hell, but hope and courage.

JOHN MURRAY

Prophets of religion are always martyred by the religious, rather than the irreligious.

REINHOLD NIEBUHR

To be religious is not to feel, but to be.

REINHOLD NIEBUHR

True religion is the life we lead, not the creed we profess.

LOUIS NIZER

My country is the world, and my religion is to do good.

THOMAS PAINE

To worship the prophet is simply an easy substitute for doing what the prophet asks.

CHARLES PARK

We can never be better for our religion if our neighbor be worse for it.

WILLIAM PENN

The aim of religion is not to get us into Heaven, but to get Heaven into us.

ULYSSES G. B. PIERCE

Religion is goodness with its sleeves rolled up.

MAGNUS RATTER

All profound religion is mystical.

ALBERT SCHWEITZER

Worship is awe in the presence of majesty.

CLARENCE R. SKINNER

Religion's glory is the glory of worship.

WILLARD L. SPERRY

All religion is an adventure in courage.

FREYA STARK

It is by no means true that any religion is better than none.

ARCHBISHOP WILLIAM TEMPLE

My religion is the answer to the question which I am.

PAUL TILLICH

Being religious is being unconditionally concerned whether in secular matters or religious.

PAUL TILLICH

Prayer is the sign that one is not alone.

PAUL TOURNIER

Religion without a great hope would be like an altar without a living fire.

HENRY VAN DYKE

Thinking that the guy up ahead knows what he is doing is the most dangerous religion.

KURT VONNEGUT

RELIGIOUS COMMUNITY

Church is a place where you get to practice what it means to be human.

JAMES LUTHER ADAMS

No strangers enter here—only friends who haven't met.

ANONYMOUS

Cooperation is simply religion being worked out in life.

J. HENRY CARPENTER

In all churches, individuals are better than their creeds.

WILLIAM ELLERY CHANNING

I love the silent church before the service better than all the preaching.

RALPH WALDO EMERSON

We are bound to one another by the same love of the Light.

ALFONS PAQUET

If we could understand each other, we could understand God also.

SWAMI SATYANANDA

Every lofty religious mind belongs not to the church, but to religious humanity.

ALBERT SCHWEITZER

They come to church to share God, not find God.

ALICE WALKER

The most holy bond of society is friendship.

MARY WOLLSTONECRAFT

SCIENCE

What is good science may not be good morality.

LEWIS WHITE BECK

Science without religion is lame; religion without science is blind.

ALBERT EINSTEIN

Man loves to wonder and that is the seed of his science.

RALPH WALDO EMERSON

Modern technology is highly spiritual because it seeks to relieve the hardships of life.

HU SHIH

Every time science opens another door . . . God is found standing behind it.

SARAH WILLIAM WALLACE ROSE

Art and science have been martyrs equally with religion.

WILLIAM TEMPLE

SELF AND SELF-KNOWLEDGE

All joys and tears alike are sent to give the soul fit nourishment.

SARAH FLOWER ADAMS

Be what you wish others to become.

HENRI FREDERIC AMIEL

A man wrapped up in himself makes a small package.

ANONYMOUS

To dream of the person you would like to be is to waste the person you are.

ANONYMOUS

When a man knows that he is wrong, he starts being right.

ANONYMOUS

We all make mistakes but everyone makes different mistakes.

LUDWIG VAN BEETHOVEN

. . . all you behold, tho' it appears without, it is within.

WILLIAM BLAKE

We are better able to teach others after we have learned the lessons ourselves.

CYRIL E. BRUBAKER

If you cannot find it in yourself, where will you go for it?

CHINESE PROVERB

There is one thing for which we must assume responsibility: the government of our own minds.

SAMUEL MCCHORD CROTHERS

People with self-respect have the courage of their mistakes.

JOAN DIDION

People need not think so much about what they ought to do, but they should remember what they are.

MEISTER ECKHART

Keep your eye on the functioning of your inner life and start from there.

MEISTER ECKHART

Trust thyself; every heart vibrates to that iron string.

RALPH WALDO EMERSON

What we are is God's gift to us. What we become is our gift to God.

RALPH WALDO EMERSON

Use what language you will, you can never say anything but what you are.

RALPH WALDO EMERSON

The only way to have a friend is to be one.

RALPH WALDO EMERSON

We can only be valued as we make ourselves valuable.

RALPH WALDO EMERSON

What lies behind you and what lies before you are tiny matters compared to what lies within you.

RALPH WALDO EMERSON

Never despise your handicaps.

HARRY EMERSON FOSDICK

Men's happiness depends upon their expectations.

CHARLES FRANKEL

I must depend on myself as the only constant friend.

MARGARET FULLER

I do not compete with the world. I compete with my ignorance.

SRI CHINMOY GHOSE

The longest journey is the journey inwards.

DAG HAMMARSKJÖLD

Self-knowledge may expand the understanding of other people's worlds.

DAG HAMMARSKJÖLD

In the last resort, it is by his own vision that every man must live.

W. E. HOCKING

You find in solitude only what you take to it.

JIMINEZ

Don't compromise yourself. You are all you've got.

JANIS JOPLIN

What we wish to become tomorrow begins with what we choose to be today.

RICHARD A. KELLAWAY

I want the understanding which bringeth peace.

HELEN KELLER

It is wisdom to know others; it is enlightenment to know one's self.

LAO TZU

We are not yet what we shall be, but we are growing toward it.

MARTIN LUTHER

The truth about ourselves is usually at variance with what we wish it to be.

JACK MENDELSOHN

I am the authority that governs the images I hold of myself and others.

J. SID PAULSON

In facing its terrors the self earns its victory.

MORSE PECKHAM

We often give to others advice we need ourselves.

ROY D. PHILIPS

The real voyage of discovery consists not in seeking new landscapes, but in having new eyes.

MARCEL PROUST

Give me neither poverty nor riches: feed me with food convenient for me.

PROVERBS 30:8

The desire not to be anything is the desire not to be.

AYN RAND

None of us lives to himself, and none of us dies to himself.

ROMANS 14:7

Remember, no one can make you feel inferior without your consent.

ELEANOR ROOSEVELT

A selfish victory is always destined to be an ultimate defeat.

FRANKLIN D. ROOSEVELT

Labor to cast self aside, and to live in the universal life.

JOSIAH ROYCE

Go not abroad for happiness—it is a flower blooming at your door.

MINOT SAVAGE

Each person I meet is part of my growth.

CATHARINE SCHRAMM

The worst poverty is the ignorance of one's riches.

RICHARD SEAVER

It is in the minds and hearts of men that decisive battles must be fought.

EDMUND W. SINNOTT

A man can lose his god, but he cannot lose himself.

HOMER V. SMITH

Everyone forges his inner self year after year.

ALEXANDER I. SOLZHENITSYN

No woman is required to build the world by destroying herself.

RABBI SOTER

We read the world wrong and say that it deceives us.

RABINDRANATH TAGORE

We are still being born and have as yet but a dim vision.

HENRY DAVID THOREAU

We are all sculptors and painters, and our material is our own flesh and blood and bones.

HENRY DAVID THOREAU

We are constantly invited to be what we are.

HENRY DAVID THOREAU

Always we have the wealth which we are, the beauty which lives.

ERNST TOLLER

In order to give oneself, one must first possess oneself.

PAUL TOURNIER

Common sense is not so common.

VOLTAIRE

Search thine own heart. What paineth thee in others in thyself may be.

JOHN GREENLEAF WHITTIER

In your own self lies destiny.

ELLA WHEELER WILCOX

SOCIETY AND SOCIAL STRUCTURE

Civilization is a method of living, an attitude of equal respect for all men.

JANE ADDAMS

Unless the promises of our civilization are soon fulfilled, civilization will die.

GORDON W. ALLPORT

No written law has ever been more binding than unwritten custom.

CARRIE CHAPMAN CATT

If strangers meet life begins.

E. E. CUMMINGS

A civilization is not conquered from without until it has destroyed itself within.

WILL DURANT

The things that divide the world are trivial as compared with the things that unite it.

RAYMOND FOSDICK

A civilization is to be judged by its treatment of minorities.

MOHANDAS K. GANDHI

The ideal society is not a choir singing in unison, but a symphony playing in harmony.

PETER GAY

The only basis for a nation's prosperity is a religious regard for the rights of others.

ISOCRATES

Where there is no vision, the people perish.

PROVERBS 29:18

Behold how good and pleasant it is for brethren to dwell together in unity.

PSALMS 133:1

In our best moments we rise above lines that separate people from people.

CURTIS W. REESE

If you think the world is all wrong, remember that it contains people like you.

HENRY H. SAUNDERSON

It is never too soon for a nation to save itself; it can be too late.

CHARLES E. SILBERMAN

The aim of government is not to rule by fear, but to free every person from fear.

SPINOZA

The world knows that the few are more than the many.

RABINDRANATH TAGORE

The supreme task of our generation is to give a soul to world consciousness.

PAUL WEISS

Every status quo is a prison to the human spirit.

HENRY NELSON WIEMAN

We are participants, whether we would or not, in the life of the world.

WOODROW WILSON

SUCCESS

The real measure of your wealth is how much you'd be worth if you lost all your money.

ANONYMOUS

Do not let the good things in life rob you of the best things.

MALTBIE D. BABCOCK

If riches increase, let thy mind hold pace with them.

SIR THOMAS BROWNE

Measure not the work until the day's out and the labor done.

ELIZABETH BARRETT BROWNING

Success is counted sweetest by those who ne'er succeed.

EMILY DICKINSON

What's worth succeeding in is worth failing in.

ROBERT FROST

Your success and happiness lie in you.

HELEN KELLER

TIME

Eternity is here while I was waiting for it.

ALBERT CAMUS

Time is made for man, not man for time.

THE CLOUD OF UNKNOWING

A poor life this, if, full of care, we have no time to stand and stare.

WILLIAM HENRY DAVIES

Forever is composed of nows.

EMILY DICKINSON

No man who is in a hurry is quite civilized.

WILL DURANT

Don't count time—make time count.

BERNARD GOLDNER

Nothing valuable can be lost by taking time.

ABRAHAM LINCOLN

Take time before time takes you.

RALPH RICHMOND

A life that has never an idle moment must have many a tense one.

DAVID RIESMAN

I am not afraid of tomorrow, for I have seen yesterday and I love today.

WILLIAM ALLEN WHITE

TRUTH

The truth which has made us free will in the end make us glad also.

FELIX ADLER

The surest way to lose truth is to pretend one already wholly possesses it.

GORDON W. ALLPORT

With a humble mind may we seek the truth and in gentleness of heart serve our generation.

ANONYMOUS

Consensus is not truth.

BESSMAN AND SWAZEY

Fear of truth is the father of censorship.

JOHN N. BOOTH

Seek what is true not what is desirable.

ALBERT CAMUS

Our search for the truth is as important to us as finding it.

JEANNE ARNOLD CHALEKIAN

The pursuit of truth shall set you free—even if you never catch up with it.

CLARENCE DARROW

We fear the truth only because we have not learned to love it.

A. POWELL DAVIES

Truth is such a rare thing it is delightful to tell it.

EMILY DICKINSON

Speak your truth quietly and clearly and listen to others; they, too, have their story.

MAX EHRMANN

Truth insists on being of this age and of this moment.

RALPH WALDO EMERSON

Thou shalt not bear false witness against thy neighbor.

EXODUS 20:16

We cannot know the truth unless we love it.

FRANÇOIS DE FENELON

Reality is of this world . . . truth is of the beyond.

G. PETER FLECK

Truth is the nursing mother of genius.

MARGARET FULLER

Truth, like surgery, may hurt, but it cures.

HAN SUYIN

Ye shall know the truth, and the truth shall make you free.

JOHN 8:32

The first casualty of any war, whether hot or cold, is truth.

JAMES AVERY JOYCE

Ultimate truth demands the concert of many voices.

CARL G. JUNG

We should never use the luxury of honesty to hurt another.

BILL NICHOLS

Truth has many shells.

LOUIS NIZER

Let us accept truth, even when it surprises us and alters our views.

GEORGE SAND

No idea is as bad as the evil it takes to suppress it.

J. F. SCHULMAN

It is the fate of every truth to be ridiculed before it is accepted.

ALBERT SCHWEITZER

Truth has no special time of its own. Its hour is now.

ALBERT SCHWEITZER

When we are told an old truth again we do not even remember that we once possessed it.

ALEXANDER I. SOLZHENITSYN

Whoever has walked with truth generates life.

SUMERIAN PROVERB

If you shut your door to all errors, truth will be shut out.

RABINDRANATH TAGORE

There is no shortcut to truth.

ALFRED NORTH WHITEHEAD

UNCERTAINTY

The vast ambiguity of our life is at once its deepest truth.

KARL BARTH

The most beautiful experience we can have is the mysterious.

ALBERT EINSTEIN

To moral questions there are no universal answers.

LAURA FERMI

One must still have chaos in oneself to be able to give birth to a dancing star.

FRIEDRICH NIETZSCHE

To live with courage, wisdom, and humility, we must accept uncertainty.

PETER PUTNAM

Life can never wait until all the evidence is in.

CHARLES E. SILBERMAN

He who would be free must dare to live with unanswered questions.

J. ROBERT SMUDSKI

It is better to ask some of the questions than to know all the answers.

JAMES THURBER

Where there is an unknowable there is a promise.

THORNTON WILDER

WAR

The point is not to make war humane; the point is to make it impossible.

ANONYMOUS

War does not determine who is right—only who is left.

ANONYMOUS

Many things are worth dying for, but none worth killing for.

ALBERT CAMUS

War is an invention of the human mind. The human mind can invent peace.

NORMAN COUSINS

All wars are civil wars since all men are brothers.

WILL DURANT

Wisdom is better than weapons of war.

ECCLESIASTES 9:18

To prevent war, all nations can unite without sacrifice of principle.

DWIGHT D. EISENHOWER

I will choose for heart, for spirit, but never will I choose for blood.

WILLIAM LEAST HEAT-MOON

Nation shall not lift up sword against nation, neither shall they learn war any more.

ISAIAH 2:4

War is fought over land that does not care, and issues that are forgotten.

ROBERT F. KAUFMANN

Wars are poor chisels for carving out peaceful tomorrows.

MARTIN LUTHER KING, JR.

To the eyes of reason war is the total eclipse of meaning.

ALAN MCGLASHAN

I must fight 'till I have conquered in myself what causes war.

MARIANNE MOORE

A bad peace is better than a good war.

RUSSIAN PROVERB

More progress is made by attacking problems than by attacking people.

HARRY SCHOLEFIELD

It is the death of love that evokes the love of death.

THORNTON WILDER

WILL AND DETERMINATION

Every day's a New Year's Day to do with as we will.

ANONYMOUS

The race is not always to the swift, but to those who keep running.

ANONYMOUS

Need a helping hand? Look at the end of your arm.

APPALACHIAN FOLK SAYING

It's up to you to whittle what you can with what you've got.

STEPHEN VINCENT BENET

It is the multitude of little actions which makes the great ones.

J. BALDWIN BROWN

Our greatest glory is not in never failing, but in rising every time we fall.

CONFUCIUS

To build high—dig deep.

CROSS STREET CHAPEL, MANCHESTER, ENGLAND

It is the creative potential itself in human beings that is the image of God.

MARY DALY

Let us listen to our own prayers. It is we who will make them real.

DENG MING DAO

Circumstances may be beyond the control of man. But his conduct is in his own power.

DISRAELI

It is far easier to start something than to finish it.

AMELIA EARHART

God indeed preserves the ship, but the mariner conducts it into the harbor.

ERASMUS

Little strokes fell great oaks.

BENJAMIN FRANKLIN

Human progress never rolls in on the wheels of inevitability.

MARTIN LUTHER KING, JR.

It is not bad to fall down. It is bad not to get up.

PHILIP M. LARSON, JR.

To try may be to die, but not to care is never to be born.

WILLIAM REDFIELD

The quality of our lives lies in doing and not in the done.

ROBERT ROSEN

Taking the line of least resistance is what makes rivers—and some people—so crooked.

HENRY H. SAUNDERSON

Think for yourself and you become a voice—and are no longer merely an echo.

HENRY H. SAUNDERSON

When the going gets tough, the tough get going.

HUGH W. SLOAN

Fortune is not on the side of the faint-hearted.

SOPHOCLES

We have climbed out of the dark only because a few dared to walk ahead and face the sun.

ANNA GARLIN SPENCER

An achievement is simply a dream upon which we have labored.

JOHN A. TAYLOR

The most likely way to reach a goal is to aim at some more ambitious goal beyond it.

ARNOLD J. TOYNBEE

It is not the leap at the start but the steady going on that gets there.

JOHN WANAMAKER

You cannot call a room truly dark if you know where the light switch is.

MAHARISHI MAHESH YOGI

Author Index

Every effort has been made to properly identify the authors of quotations in this book. Some identities, however, have been lost to time. If you have information to add to this index, please write to Skinner House Books, 25 Beacon Street, Boston, Massachusetts 02108-2800.

Butler, Samuel (1835-1902), English novelist and essayist, 27

Buxton, Charles (1823-1871), English politician, 45

C

Caldwell, Taylor (1900-1985), English-born American novelist, 31

Call, Lon Ray (1894-1985), minister-at-large for the American Unitarian Association (1941-1951), 79

Camara, Dom Helder (1909-), Brazilian Roman Catholic theologian and prelate, 54, 62

Campbell, Sara Moores (1943-), Unitarian Universalist minister and author, 25

Camus, Albert (1913-1960), French novelist, essayist, and playwright, 21, 30, 40, 96, 98, 102

Carlisle, Thomas (1795-1881), British historian and social critic of early Victorian England, 62

Carnes, Paul (1921-1979), 3rd president of the Unitarian Universalist Association (1977-1979), 49, 70

Carpenter, J. Henry, 83

Carrier, Gaston M. (1920-), Unitarian Universalist minister, 43

Cary, (Arthur) Joyce (1888-1957), English novelist, 36

Cary, Alice (1820-1871), American poet and co-founder of Sorosis, a women's literary group, 62

Cary, Phoebe (1824-1871), American poet and co-founder of Sorosis, a women's literary group, 67

Castillo, Michel Del (1933-), French novelist, 45

Cather, Willa (1873-1947), American author of mid-western prairie life, 67

Cato, Marcus Porcius (234-149 BCE), Roman soldier, politician, orator, and author, 14

Catt, Carrie Chapman (1859-1947), American reformer and founder of the League of Women Voters, 93

Cervantes, Miguel de (1547-1616), Spanish author, 40

Cox, Harvey (1929-), American theology professor, 79

Cross Street Chapel, Manchester, England (founded 1662), site of the first Wayside Pulpit in England, established December 26, 1920 by the Reverend H. Harrold Johnson, 105

Crothers, Samuel McChord (1857-1927), Unitarian minister and American essayist, 79, 86

cummings, e. e. (1894-1962), American poet, 93

Curie, Marie (1867-1934), Polish-born French physicist, 63

D

Daly, Mary, (1928-), American feminist, theological writer, and philosopher, 105

Darrow, Clarence (1857-1938), American labor and criminal lawyer, 98

Dávid, Francis (1510-1579), Hungarian minister and court preacher to King John Sigismund of Transylvania, established Unitarianism in Transylvania in 1568, 31

Davies, A. Powell (1902-1957), Unitarian minister who spoke openly for civil rights and against McCarthyism, 30, 43, 98

Davies, William Henry (1871-1940), Welsh poet, 96

Dawson, Marshall, 31

Debs, Eugene V. (1855-1926), American union organizer, 55

Deng Ming Dao, Chinese Taoist scholar and author, 105

Desmahis, 55

Dewar, Thomas, 58

Dewey, John (1859-1952), American educator, 58

Dhammapada, anthology of 423 Buddhist verses, 45

Dickinson, Emily (1830-1886), American poet, 95, 96, 98

Diderot, Denis (1713-1784), French philosopher, playwright, and novelist, 33

Didion, Joan (1934-), American writer of contemporary social tensions, 86

Ellis, Havelock (1859-1939), English physician and writer, 47, 63

Emerson, Ralph Waldo (1803-1882), American writer, poet, and ordained Unitarian minister, 15, 20, 21, 23, 26, 27, 30, 35, 41, 43, 58, 83, 84, 87, 98

Epictetus (ca. 50-135 CE), Greek philosopher, 63

Erasmus, Desiderius (1466-1536), Dutch scholar and leader of the humanist movement, 105

Erikson, Erik H. (1902-1994), German-born American psycholanalyst and educator, 47

Euripides (480-406 BCE), Greek playwright, 38, 44

Eusebius (ca. 264-340 CE), theologian and scholar, probably born in Palestine, 75

F

Fahs, Sophia Lyon (1876-1978), Unitarian religious educator ordained in 1959, 25

Fenelon, François de (1651-1715), French prelate, theologian, and preacher, 99

Fenn, William Wallace, 79

Ferm, Deane William, 77

Fermi, Laura (1907-1977), Italian-born American scientist of atomic energy, 101

Finney, Charles G. (1792-1875), American Presbyterian minister, theologian, and educator, 79

Fleck, G. Peter (1909-1995), international banker and venture capitalist who became a Unitarian Universalist minister at age 75, 99

Foerster, L. Annie (1935-), Unitarian Universalist minister, 47

Fosdick, Harry Emerson (1878-1969), American Protestant preacher and pacifist, 87

Fosdick, Raymond (1883-1972), American lawyer and politician, 93

Gould, Cynthia J., 49

Grayson, David (1870-1946), American journalist and writer, 19

Greeley, Dana McLean (1908-1986), president of the American Unitarian Association (1958-1961) and first president of the Unitarian Universalist Association (1961-1969), 55

Grenfell, Sir Wilfred Thomason (1865-1940), English physician and missionary, 64

Gunther, John (1901-1970), American author and journalist, 59

H

Half, Robert (1918-), American entrepreneur, 15

Hallman, Laurel (1943-), Unitarian Universalist minister, 80

Hammarskjöld, Dag (1905-1961), Swedish diplomat and secretary general of the United Nations (1953-1961), 15, 75, 88

Han Suyin (1917-), Chinese-born British novelist, 99

Hayward, John F. (1916-1983), English art historian, 36

Hazlitt, William (1778-1830), English literalist, social critic, and part-time painter, 53

Head, Geoffrey, 35

Heat-Moon, William Least (1939-), American writer and traveler of the American mid-west, 103

Hegel, Georg Wilhelm Friedrich (1770-1831), German philosopher and educator, 38

Heinemann, Frederick H., 49

Helverson, Ralph (1912-), retired Unitarian Universalist minister, 19

Heraclitus (active ca. 500 BCE), Greek philosopher, 23

Herbert, George (1593-1633), English metaphysical poet and Anglican priest, 70

James, William (1842-1910), American philosopher and psychologist, 64

Jauves, Jean, 59

Jefferson, Thomas (1743-1826), American philosopher, political leader, author of the Declaration of Independence, and 3rd president of the US (1801-1809), 44, 77, 80

Jiminez, Juan Ramon (1881-1958), Spanish symbolist poet, 88

Jinnah, Mohammad Ali (1876-1948), political leader and first governor general of Pakistan (1947-1948), 75

Johnson, H. Harrold, English Unitarian minister and creator of the first Wayside Pulpit in England, December 26, 1920, 8

Johnston, J. Donald, 33, 71

Jones, Mary Harris "Mother" (1830-1930), Irish immigrant who devoted her life to improving conditions for the working class, 18

Jones, Rufus M. (1863-1948), American Quaker philosopher, historian, and social reformer, 80

Jones, Sir William (1746-1794), English jurist and Asian scholar, 16

Joplin, Janis (1943-1970), American rock singer, 88

Joseph, Morris, 64

Joubert, Joseph (1754-1824), French writer and moralist, 16, 25

Joyce, James Avery (1882-1941), Irish novelist, 99

Jung, Carl (1875-1961), Swiss psychologist and psychiatrist, 16, 21, 33, 99

K

Kaiser, Henry J. (1882-1967), American industrialist and creator of the largest private health plan in 1942, 17

Kaufmann, Robert F. (1921-), Unitarian Universalist minister, 103

Kellaway, Richard A. (1934-), Unitarian Universalist minister, 88

Lindeman, Eduard (1885-1953), American Danish philosopher and educator, 17

Lippman, Walter (1889-1974), American author and independent thinker, 51

Locke, John (1632-1704), English philosopher and political theorist, 17

Longfellow, Henry Wadsworth (1807-1882), American poet, 41

Luther, Martin (1483-1546), German reformer and preacher, 89

Lynch, William, 49

M

McGlashan, Alan, 103

Madison, Orin E., 17

Maggio, Rosalie, American writer and editor of quotation collections and grammar reference texts, 11

Maharishi Mahesh Yogi (1911-), Indian guru, missionary of traditional Indian thought, and founder of the Transcendental Meditation Movement, 107

Malraux, Andre (1901-1976), French writer, existentialist, and politician, 33

Marshall, Peter (1902-1949), Scottish-born American Presbyterian minister, 17

Martin, Everett Dean (1880-1941), Unitarian minister and liberal educator, 60

Martineau, Harriet (1802-1876), English abolitionist and writer of positivistic philosophy, 80

Masaryk, Tomas Garrigue (1850-1937), Czech philosopher and first president of Czechoslovakia (1918-1935), 80

Masefield, John (1878-1967), English journalist, poet, and novelist, 47

Mead, Margaret (1901-1978), American anthropologist, 60, 80

N

O

P

Q

R

Rose, W. W., 39

Rose, William Wallace, 85

Rosen, Robert, 106

Ross, Floyd, 65

Royce, Josiah (1855-1916), American philosopher, 90

Royce, Sir Henry (1863-1933), English engineer and co-founder of Rolls-Royce (1906), 27

Rudolph, Frederick, 33

Ruskin, John (1819-1900), English critic and social theorist, 65

Russell, Bertrand (1872-1970), British mathematician, philosopher, and social reformer, 28, 60

Russell, Rollo, 76

S

Sagan, Carl (1934-1996), American astronomer, 48

Saint-Exupéry, Antoine-Marie-Roger de (1900-1944), French novelist, essayist, and commercial pilot, 69

Sand, George (1804-1876), French novelist, 100

Sandburg, Carl (1878-1967), American poet, journalist, and singer, 25

Santayana, George (1863-1952), Spanish and American philosopher, 30, 37, 61

Sarton, May (1912-), Belgian-born American poet and writer, 24

Sartre, Jean-Paul (1905-1980), French philosopher, writer, and Existentialist, 22

Satchidananda, Swami (1914-), Indian-born yoga master and spiritual leader, 76

Satyananda, Swami, German former journalist and disciple of Guru Oshu, 52, 84

Saunderson, Henry Hallam (1871-1957), American Unitarian minister who introduced the Wayside Community Pulpit to North America, 7, 8, 10, 24, 94, 106

Shute, Nevil (1899-1960), English novelist, 48

Sidney, Sir Philip (1554-1586), English poet, courtier, diplomat, and soldier, 24

Silberman, Charles E. (1925-), American sociologist and author, 94, 101

Simpson, George (1902-1984), American paleontologist, 35

Sinnott, Edmund W. (1888-1968), American botanist and educator, 91

Sittler, Joseph (1904-1987), American theologian, educator, and author, 57

Skinner, Clarence R. (1881-1949), Universalist theologian and minister, founder of the Community Church in Boston (1920), and dean of Crane Theological School at Tufts College (1933-1945), 82

Sloan, Hugh W. (1941-), American treasurer for Richard Nixon's re-election campaign, 106

Smith, Elizabeth Oakes (1806-1893), American author, lecturer, and reformer, 35

Smith, Homer V., 91

Smith, Lillian (1897-1966), American Southern writer and critic of racism, 34

Smudski, J. Robert, 101

Solzhenitsyn, Alexander I. (1918-), Soviet novelist imprisoned for criticizing Stalin, 91, 100

Sophocles (496-406 BCE), Greek playwright and poet who wrote of humanism, 42, 106

Soter, Rabbi, 91

Spencer, Anna Garlin (1851-1931), American Unitarian transcendentalist and reformer, 107

Sperry, Willard L. (1882-1954), American Protestant cleric and theologian, 82

Spinoza, Baruch (1632-1677), Dutch philosopher and theorist in the rationalist tradition, 94

T

Terence (ca. 195-159 BCE), Roman comic dramatist, 57

Teresa, Mother (1910-1997), Roman Catholic nun and missionary, 18

Thomas, Lewis (1913-1993), American physician, author, and educator, 50

Thoreau, Henry David (1817-1862), American author and transcendentalist, 19, 29, 39, 65, 66, 73, 91

Thurber, James (1894-1961), American writer and artist, 71, 102

Thurman, Howard (1900-1981), African American theologian and religious leader, 24, 35, 71

Tillich, Paul (1886-1965), German-American Protestant theologian and philosopher, 42, 82

Toller, Ernst (1893-1939), German playwright and expressionist, 92

Tolstoy, Leo (1828-1910), Russian novelist and moral philosopher, 25, 69

Tournier, Paul (1898-1986), Swiss physician and writer, 82, 92

Toynbee, Arnold J. (1889-1972), English historian and philosopher, 61, 66, 107

Turner, J. E., 40

Tutu, Desmond (1931-), Anglican archbishop and anti-apartheid leader in South Africa, 40

Twain, Mark (1835-1910), American novelist, 22

U

Unamuno y Jugo, Miguel de (1864-1936), Spanish philosopher, writer, and early exponent of Existentialism, 22

Ustinov, Peter (1921-), British actor and playwright, 29, 37

V

Van Buren, Abigail (1918-), American advice columnist, 19